The Life of
Saint Brigid

First published in 2007 by
Appletree Press Ltd
The Old Potato Station
14 Howard Street South
Belfast
BT7 1AP

Tel: +44 (0) 28 90 24 30 74
Fax: +44 (0) 28 90 24 67 56
E-mail: reception@appletree.ie
Web: www.appletree.ie

The Life of Saint Brigid

ISBN-13: 978 0 86281 999 6
ISBN-10: 0 86281 999 7

Desk & Marketing Editor: Jean Brown
Editorial Work: Jim Black
Designer: Stuart Wilkinson
Production Manager: Paul McAvoy

9 8 7 6 5 4 3 2 1

AP3321

The Life of
Saint Brigid

Anna Egan Smucker

Appletree Press

Dedication

*For Linda who said this story had to be told,
and for all of my Irish relatives –
the Egans, Conlons, Malloys, McGills, Connors, and Caniffs*

Contents

Introduction   7

Chapter 1   The Story of St Brigid   9

Chapter 2   Brigid – Goddess and Saint   35

Chapter 3   St Brigid's Day Folk Customs   41

Chapter 4   St Brigid the Aid-Woman   48

Chapter 5   Traditional Prayers to St Brigid   53

Chapter 6   St Brigid Today   61

Chapter 7   Making a St Brigid's Cross   65

Sources   69

Acknowledgements   71

Introduction

The first of February, the first day of the Irish spring, is celebrated as St Brigid's Feast Day. Who was this woman who, along with Patrick and Columcille, is one of the three great patron saints of Ireland? Legends of the saint tell of an *extraordinary* woman who lived in the fifth and sixth centuries at the very beginning of Christianity in Ireland. She was a healer of the sick, a counsellor of bishops, and a peacemaker in a violent time. She was the founder of a renowned monastery – *Cill Dara* (Church of the Oak) on the Hill of Kildare. Above all, she was merciful to the poor.

February 1st was also the time of the pre-Christian Celtic celebration of *Imbolc*, when seeds were sown and lambs were born. It is not surprising that underlying, and often mixing with the legends of the saint, is another story – the story of a goddess who had the same name. Brigid, the triple goddess, was goddess of poetry, smith-work, and healing; and goddess of nurturing, fertility, and fire.

The legends of the saint are infused with stories of the goddess and it is impossible to separate one from the other. The recounting of signs and wonders in the story of St Brigid has its own kind of truth, deeper than the literal. Perhaps it is not too great a stretch to imagine that the goddess would be pleased with her namesake who saw the face of God in all those in need and who held the earth and all its creatures sacred.

Saint Brigid and her cloak

Chapter One
The Story of St Brigid

In Ireland, long ago, people worshipped all that surrounded them: water, wind, earth, air, and the sun. Everywhere, gods and goddesses inhabited the world. One could never be certain of what might please them or provoke their anger. Plagues wiped out whole families. Lightning struck thatched roofs and houses burned to the ground. Survivors were left to wonder what taboos had been unknowingly broken, what saving rituals might have been performed. Feuding tribes battled across the countryside. Life for most was short and hard. It seemed that even the dark clouds struggled with the sun to prevail.

Then from across the Irish Sea came men bearing word of a god who was God of all the elements and all creation. One of these men was named Patrick. He walked the land preaching the news of this one God. At the wells sacred to the gods and goddesses of the old religion, he made the sign of the Cross, blessing the water in the name of God who was Father, Son, and Spirit. Those who came to listen to Patrick heard a message of love, forgiveness, and hope. And many asked to be baptised, to become followers of this God, whose light, stronger than a million suns, would last forever.

When Patrick was in the province of Leinster, preaching about this God in whose eyes all were equal, he baptised many women slaves. One was named Broicseach, the slave of a local chieftain named Dubhthach*. She was as beautiful as she was kind, and her master fell in love with her. It was not long before Broicseach was carrying his child. Dubhthach's wife, jealous of Broicseach from the first time she saw her, ordered her husband to sell the slave to a far-off land. But Dubhthach loved the slave-woman and refused to do that.

*Broicseach pronounced Brocksheh; Dubhthach pronounced Duffach

9

One day as he and Broicseach drove into the countryside in his chariot, they passed the house of a learned man, a druid. When this man heard the rumble of the wheels, he knew, in the way the wise have of telling, that a person of great importance was passing by, and he sent his servant out to see who it was. When the servant returned, saying that it was only Dubhthach, the wise man went out to see for himself. After greeting the chieftain, he inquired of the woman who stood by his side. On learning that she carried Dubhthach's child, the old man prophesied that the child would be a daughter whose life and work would shine like the sun among the stars. At this amazing news, Dubhthach became more determined than ever to keep his beautiful slave.

Weeks later, two bishops were passing Dubhthach's house. Even though Dubhthach was not a follower of the new religion, the rules of hospitality required that he make them welcome. When Broicseach entered the room, carrying food and drink, the bishops made the same wondrous prophecy about her child as the druid had done. By this time, Dubhthach's wife was in a rage. The bishops, knowing there would be no peace in the household until Broicseach was gone, advised Dubhthach to sell the slave, but not the daughter who was to be so renowned. And that is what Dubhthach regretfully did.

The person who bought Broicseach was a druid named Colman. He was a kind master, but Broicseach was still required to work tending the cows. As the months went by, the weight of the buckets and the exertion of churning the milk into butter left her exhausted and weak.

One morning, just as the first streaks of dawn were reddening the sky, Broicseach carried the buckets of warm milk toward the dairy. The yoke cut into her shoulders as she turned sideways to carry her load through the narrow doorway, and there on the threshold, neither within nor without, Broicseach gave birth to the long-awaited baby girl. The other women set down their buckets and rushed to help. Some tended the mother while the oldest of the women washed the baby with the warm milk. The child, unusually fair for one so new, gazed at the flickering light of the torches and stretched wide her perfect arms. Then the women swaddled her in the softest cloth that could be found, and laid her in the arms of her mother.

If Broicseach doubted the prophecies that had been made concerning her daughter, she did not have long to wait for a sign of the child's extraordinary nature. When her baby was a few months old, Broicseach left her sound asleep in the house and went out to look after a cow. Soon after she left, labourers in a nearby field looked up to see the house on fire, the flames towering into the sky. But as they rushed toward it, the fire suddenly disappeared. In the house, they found not even the smell of smoke. The baby slept peacefully in her bed. The labourers left quietly, wondering if their eyes had somehow deceived them.

The druid, Colman, had not been baptised into the new religion that Broicseach followed, but one morning he came to her telling of a dream he had had during the night.

"I saw three angels," he said. "They were dressed in white and were pouring oil on the child's head in the way bishops of your religion baptise. One of the angels turned to me and said, 'this shall be the child's name: Brigid.'"

Broicseach took her baby in her arms and said, "The angels have named you, my little child. *Brigid* you shall be."

After this, Colman felt a special kinship toward the child. When it was time for her to be weaned, he became concerned when she could not eat the porridge commonly given to children her age. He scoured the countryside until he found a white red-eared cow, and on that milk, the child Brigid flourished.

She especially loved the spring. When the dark winter finally ended, she danced barefoot in the silky new grass and called back to the birds singing in the trees as if she knew their secret language. Only the smell of oatcakes baking on the fire could entice her indoors. Her work was to help care for the sheep, finding the ones that strayed, and comforting the lambs that had lost their mothers. When the air turned cool, she sat in the midst of the flock and rubbed their warm fleece as the sheep nuzzled against her.

The druid found in Brigid an eager student, and he taught her the plants that healed. "Tell me, now," he said, "which of these cures the ache in the stomach?"

And Brigid snatched up the plant with the clusters of yellow flowers.

"And which can stop the flow of blood?"

"The plant with the stinging leaves."

"And how can we find water?"

"With the branches of the willow."

"And the name of this tree?"

"Hazel."

"And what bird is that plummeting from the sky?"

"A merlin?"

Hungrily she listened to his tales of heroes like Cuchulainn and Finn, stories of courage and betrayal, of battles lost and won.

From her mother, Brigid learned not only to tend, but to love, the animals. She learned to milk the cows and make the butter, to spin wool into thread, and how to make the bread and ale. From her mother, who had been baptised and taught by Saint Patrick himself, she also learned of the loving, merciful God in whose sight slaves were the same as kings, and who, like a good shepherd, cared for the flock, especially the hurt and the lost. Brigid took to heart all the stories of this loving God and a longing began to grow in her to serve Him. When the poor came to her door, she fed them. And, even during the times when Brigid and her mother barely had enough to eat, no one went away hungry. At night, she and her mother knelt before a cross, plaited from rushes, and prayed to this Good Shepherd.

As she grew older, Brigid also began to long to see Dubhthach, the father she had never known. And, when she was no longer a child, but a young woman, she asked to be allowed to go to him. A message was sent, and in due time, Dubhthach came for her. Brigid had never seen anyone so grandly dressed, nor been in a chariot so polished and plumed.

Admiring the sleek, spirited horses, she couldn't keep herself from asking, "Father, may I drive them?'

Somewhat reluctantly, he handed over the reins. "Careful, now," he said as the chariot leapt forward. The wind lifted her golden hair and she laughed in delight as the horses galloped faster and faster.

They hadn't gone far, when a woman accompanying them fell ill. Dubhthach sent Brigid and another young girl to a house where a man was having a great feast to ask for some refreshment.

"Please, sir, a drink of ale for a sick woman," Brigid said.

"A likely story…Go away!" he shouted.

Brigid filled a bucket out of a nearby well.

She blessed it "In the name of God the Father, the Son, and the Holy Spirit," and said, "Father of us all, there is a woman in need." And from the water, rose the smell of ale.

Upon drinking it, the sick woman was healed, while at the banquet not a drop of ale was to be found.

Told what had happened, Brigid's father, amazed, said nothing, but as they drove on, he recalled the druid's prophecy so long ago, and pondered Colman's account of how everything Brigid set her hand to had flourished. Anticipating a like effect, when they reached his home he put her in charge of his household.

Brigid was astonished at his wealth – a home with soft cushions and bright wall hangings, the fine garments and the gold and silver jewellery of her father and his wife, the great number of cows, sheep, swine, and geese…so much to be owned by one person. And Brigid was to manage it. She would follow her heart in doing that.

All seemed to be going well until one day when Brigid's father was entertaining guests. He cut a piece of bacon into five pieces and gave it to her to cook. Now when Brigid was boiling the bacon, a starving hound came into her kitchen. Moved by his

pitiful whimpering, she gave the animal one of the pieces. When the dog wolfed it down and looked up at her expectantly, she gave him another piece. All this time, one of the guests had been secretly watching, and he reported to Brigid's father what he had seen.

As she was finishing the meal preparations, her father came to her and asked, "Have you boiled the bacon?"

"Yes, Father," she said.

"And tell me, do all the portions remain?"

"Count them," she replied.

And her father counted them – five in number.

Whether the guests thought the food tainted by magic, or too holy for them to eat, we do not know, but they would eat none of it. Brigid was more than happy to give it to the poor. And they began to come in increasing numbers to her kitchen door.

As time went on, her father scarcely knew what to think of his daughter. He was no believer in this new God, in whose name she seemed to be giving away his entire larder. But when he counted his provisions, they were all there. In fact, his animals had never been so fertile, nor his harvest so abundant. He didn't like what he couldn't understand, and Brigid was like no young woman he had ever known.

Now when Brigid had been in her father's house for some time, she began to yearn to see her mother who was still enslaved in Connacht. She had never been strong and Brigid began to feel uneasy about her health. So one day she asked Dubhthach if she might go visit her mother. Seeing this as an opportunity to assert his authority, he refused. Disregarding him, Brigid threw on her cloak, grabbed a walking stick, and set off. She would go by foot, without her father's chariot, and without his consent.

Days later, her feet blistered and sore, Brigid arrived at her old home. Told that her mother was tending the cows in a nearby pasture, she rushed to her side. Shocked at how sickly and frail her mother looked, Brigid helped her to her bed. Returning to the pasture, Brigid took her mother's place.

And so it was that Brigid set to work again in the house of Colman the druid, milking cows and churning butter. Always, she divided the first churning into twelve shares in honour of the twelve apostles. She set aside a thirteenth portion, greater than the rest, in honour of Christ, and this she gave to the poor.

When Colman asked the herdsman how Brigid was faring, he suggested the druid go to see for himself. So Colman sent word to Brigid that she should churn enough butter to fill a basket eight fists in height. When he went to see if she had done the work, she had churned only a small amount. She went in and out of the room repeating this prayer:

O God, O my Prince
Who can do all these things,
Bless, O God
With thy right hand this kitchen.
May Mary's Son, my Friend, come
To bless my kitchen.
The Prince of all the world,
May we have abundance with Him.

Each time she brought a half churning and soon the large basket was filled.

It was in this way that the druid Colman came to know Brigid's God. He offered Brigid the butter as well as the cows she had been milking and said, "You shall not live as a slave to me. Your true work is to serve the Lord."

She asked only that her mother be freed. At this, the druid gave her everything. Brigid, in turn, gave the butter, the milk, as well as the cows to the poor. Then Brigid took her mother to her own people, and she returned to Dubhthach's house.

It was with mixed feelings that Brigid's father and his wife received her. The young lady who had picked up her walking stick and left them had returned a beautiful young woman. Her blonde hair, tamed into a braid, now reached all the way down her back to touch her slender waist. She seemed quieter than they remembered. Older and wiser, they hoped.

The summer grass grew lush and thick in Dubhthach's pasture where Brigid sat watching the animals. She knew it would not be long before her father would expect her to marry. Wouldn't she prefer a necklace of daisies to a torque of gold, a bank of emerald moss to a cushion of velvet? Weren't the reds and purples of the sunset richer than the colours of any king's cloak? No chieftain's riches could compare with these. Look at the lilies of the field. Didn't the Lord himself say that? And didn't he give away everything – even his life? She would find a way to give her life to him. In the days that followed, her desire to serve this Lord grew from a steady flame into an all-consuming fire.

Soon Dubhthach and his wife could barely get in and out the door for all the beggars crowded there. Dubhthach's wife, who was as jealous of Brigid and her beauty as she had been of Brigid's mother, urged her husband to sell Brigid into slavery. When Dubhthach saw Brigid give away his favourite cloak, he decided the time had come to do just that.

Dubhthach asked Brigid to come out in his chariot. As he whipped his horses to go faster, Dubhthach turned to his daughter and said, "You are not riding in my chariot as a sign of honour. I intend to sell you to the King."

"Father!" Brigid grabbed her father's hand, and almost fell as the chariot clattered over a large stone.

Unmoved, Dubhthach continued, "You will be a slave in King Dunlang MacEnda's house, turning his grinding wheels."

Brigid could do nothing but hang on as her father raced his chariot over the bumpy road. When they arrived at the King's fortress, he hurried in, leaving her to sit in the chariot at the door. Brigid looked at his sword, left, as custom demanded, outside the King's walls. Its hilt, inlaid with amber, was one of her father's treasured possessions.

A leper, who had been watching all of this, wrapped his rags around himself and came up to Brigid. Holding out his diseased hands, he begged, "Please, good lady, alms?" She had nothing to give him. The only thing in the chariot that was of any value was her father's sword. To refuse the leper was to refuse Christ. Wasn't the leper's face the Lord's face? Brigid hesitated a moment, then picked up the sword. With hands that she willed not to tremble, she held it out to the leper, saying: "Take it. Sell it for food."

Inside the fortress, the King had asked that Brigid be brought to him. Her father exploded into rage when he discovered that, in his short absence, she had given away his valued sword. He hauled her by her hair into the fortress.

The King, knowing her past and learning what she had just done, asked, "Will you also take my wealth and my cattle and give them to the poor?"

Brigid took a deep breath and began, "The Lord knows if I had all your land in Leinster, and all your wealth…" she paused. Then meeting his gaze, she continued, "Yes, I would give everything to the poor in His name."

"Brigid!" her father shouted, and raised his arm to strike her, but the King held him back. As a Christian himself, Dunlang MacEnda understood her better than her father.

"We are not fit to bargain about this maiden," he said, and motioned for his servant. "Her worth is surely greater before God than ours."

And the King gave Brigid's father an ivory-hilted sword to replace the one she had given away, and sent Brigid home again a free woman.

Her father, refusing to even look at her, resolved that she would not give away even a stale crust of his bread. He was determined to be rid of her by marrying her off. Perhaps her beauty would make up for her other faults. So it was with great relief that he, and his sons, greeted a nobleman who had come to ask for Brigid in marriage. But Brigid refused this suitor as well as all the others that would follow.

Beccan, one of her half-brothers, taunted her saying, "What good is the fair eye that does not look across the pillow at a husband?"

Brigid put her finger under her eye and pulled it out of her head saying, "Here, then, is your fair eye, Beccan."

At last recognising that it was useless to try to bend her to his will, her father said, "O daughter, put a veil on your head. If you have dedicated yourself to your God, I will no longer try to snatch you from him."

Brigid put her palm to her eye and it was healed. So with her father's permission, if not his blessing, Brigid gathered around her eight other women who also wanted to dedicate their lives to God. Together they travelled to Meath to Bishop Mel to take the vows that would wed them to Christ as nuns.

There, Brigid waited for the other women to precede her so that she might go last, but that was not to be. The darkness was lit up by a tongue of flame that rose from her head all the way up to the ridgepole of the church. Bishop Mel asked who she was.

MacCaille, another bishop, said, "That, *that* is Brigid."

"Come, O holy Brigid," said Bishop Mel, "that the veil may be placed on your head before the others."

Then an extraordinary thing happened. Instead of saying the words that would consecrate Brigid a nun, Bishop Mel pronounced the words that ordained her a bishop. MacCaille immediately protested that no woman could become a bishop.

But Mel, seeing in this event the working of the Holy Spirit, said, "God has given her this honour, not me."

As she was being consecrated, Brigid grasped the beam that supported the altar. At her touch, the wood that was dry and dead became wood that was green and growing.

Instead of returning to their homes to live prayerful lives as was the custom, Brigid resolved that she and the other young women would live in community, praying together and performing works of mercy. Just as she had always tended to the physical needs of the people around her, so she would continue. And now, not only free, but consecrated to a life of serving God, her energy knew no bounds.

As it was the time of Easter, she wanted all to rejoice in body as well as spirit. Single-minded in her trust that God could do all things, she set about to brew ale for all the churches in the area, even though the corn harvest that year had been poor and she had only one measure of malt. Having only two troughs, Brigid and the nuns made a tub of one of them and filled the other with ale. The nuns kept taking the ale from Brigid to the churches, and still the trough before Brigid remained full. The one measure of malt, through Brigid's blessing, supplied seven churches with

Bishop Mel

the finest ale for Maundy Thursday and through the eight days of Easter.

Many stories are told of how Brigid healed the sick. Just as the Lord had done, Brigid washed the feet of the old and sick who came to a church near her community. When she washed the feet of a crippled man, a madman, a blind man, and a leper they were healed. Once Brigid was a guest in a house where there lived a young man of fourteen years who had never spoken, nor moved. Now Brigid didn't know this, and when more people arrived at the house, she asked him to tend to the guests. He got up and served them and was whole from that day on.

As her own mother had lived in bondage, Brigid worked tirelessly to free those who were enslaved, travelling the land to plead with chieftains and kings to free those imprisoned unjustly. One of these was a man who, while he was cutting firewood, killed a fox, not knowing that it was a pet of the King of Leinster. Now this fox was dearer to the King than any of his dogs, and, with its ability to perform many tricks, was a favourite at court. Shaking with anger, the King ordered the man seized and thrown into prison.

As Brigid drove her chariot through the woods to try to ransom the man, she happened to see a wild fox. Calling to it, she motioned for it to come to her. With one leap it landed in her chariot and nestled under her cloak. When they arrived at the King's fortress, Brigid introduced the fox to the King and announced that even though nothing could replace his pet, this

fox was certainly as smart and talented. Immediately, the fox played and performed tricks as well as the pet that had been killed, and the King was appeased. After Brigid and the freed man departed, the fox, smart animal that he was, escaped back into the woods eluding the King's soldiers who chased after him on foot, on horse, and with their baying hounds.

On another occasion a man, who had clumsily dropped and broken a gem-encrusted cup which belonged to the King, was jailed and sentenced to death. Bishop Mel pleaded for the man's release, but the King would not change his mind. The cup, exquisite in its craftsmanship, was one of his treasures. The bishop, in desperation, asked for the pieces of the cup and a day's stay of the man's execution. Calling for his chariot, the bishop raced to Brigid. She took the sack containing the fragments and disappeared into her little church. Holding the pieces in her hands, she prayed to the Lord that the poor man's life might be saved. When she emerged from the darkness of the church, the sun's rays lit up the jewelled cup, restored to a form even more beautiful than its original. Bishop Mel returned it to the King saying, "Not for me has God worked this miracle, but for Brigid." And so the captive was set free.

One day toward the end of a hard winter, Brigid went to a chieftain's fortress to seek the release of a prisoner only to be told that the chieftain was away. Now she and her nuns had travelled far, and they were cold and wet. The chieftain's brother told them they were welcome to wait for his brother's return, but added that it was unlikely he would set his prisoner free.

"I am prepared to wait," Brigid said, moving toward the fire. The chieftain's foster-sons exchanged looks. This promised to be a real contest of wills. Their foster-father was a stern man, not known for forgiving those he felt had wronged him.

After warming themselves and enjoying the food and drink that was set before them, Brigid and her nuns settled down to wait. It was then that Brigid, who loved music, noticed the harps hanging on the walls.

"Please, could someone play for us?" she asked. "Surely it would lift all our spirits on such a dark day."

The elderly foster-father of the chieftain roused himself from a half-sleep. "Our harpist is absent and, sadly, no one here knows how to play," he said, a dry cough rattling in his chest.

One of Brigid's nuns walked over to the foster-son who had brought them cups of mulled wine. "Please, why don't you try," she said. "Many things that seem impossible are not so when done for Brigid."

The young man, wanting to be hospitable, obliged. Taking down one of the harps, he hesitantly began to strum. Before long, he was playing melodies so wonderful that his brother was inspired to take down the second harp and play. The chieftain, nearing his fortress, was amazed at the sounds coming from his home. As he entered the hall where Brigid sat, music and merriment enveloped him. And most welcome to his ears, was the laughter of his ailing foster-father. With his heart so moved, he couldn't help but agree to release his prisoner to Brigid.

The days that she travelled the land were violent ones, and she did everything in her power to stop the killing, to make peace. Once the King of Leinster himself came to worship with Brigid and her community on Easter-day. When Mass was over, the King rode off to lead his army into battle. Brigid, unhappy that she had been unable to stop the King, went to preside at the dinner. Lomman, a leper, sat, as always, beside her. On this holiest of days, one that should have been filled with rejoicing, he knew what saddened Brigid. As the food and drink were served, Lomman refused everything.

"Are you not feeling well, Lomman?" Brigid asked.

"As with you," he said, "it is my heart not my stomach that aches. I have vowed to fast until the King's weapons are brought to me."

And he wanted all of it – spears, sword, and shield. To deny the leper was to deny Christ. Brigid gladly sent a messenger after the King.

The King, nearing the place where he knew his enemy was encamped, pretended not to hear the request. From midday until evening, a thick fog descended on him, and he could not find his way. From the moment the messenger told of Lomman's fast, the King's army did not advance even one thousand paces. The fog did not lift until the weapons were given to the messenger, and, with Brigid's blessing, bestowed on the leper. On that day, at least, no blood was shed.

Brigid knew, without seeing, when a battle was raging. Once when Bishop Erc was visiting, she told him that a battle was being fought between his tribe and its neighbours. A student travelling with the bishop contradicted her, saying, "That is not true." Brigid said nothing, but asking him to close his eyes, she made on them the sign of the cross. The student's brow furrowed in pain, and he said, "Yes, now I see my brothers slaughtering each other." And so he repented, becoming a peacemaker himself once he had seen the bloodshed as Brigid saw it.

As a fire in the darkness attracts those who are cold or lost, more and more people came to Brigid to join her in her work. The King had promised Brigid land on which to build a dwelling place and church, but he was in no hurry to give it to her. Finally, he agreed to meet.

It was a beautiful morning in May. The King was in high spirits. "Now, Brigid," he said, "what land would you have of me?"

The land Brigid wanted was rich grassland and a ridge with a commanding view of the Liffey plain. The King was not likely to grant it to her. Praying that God would give her words to sway the King, she was surprised to hear herself say, "I would have the land that my cloak might cover."

The King laughingly agreed. But his laughter turned to stunned disbelief as four of Brigid's nuns took the corners of her cloak and began to run, each to one of the four directions with the expanding cloak billowing behind them.

Fearing that the cloak would cover all of Leinster, the King cried out, "Brigid! Order your nuns to stop! You will have your land."

The lush meadow became known as Brigid's Pastures.

When Brigid was ready to build her monastery, it happened that Ailill, the King's son, was passing nearby with a hundred horses loaded down with peeled logs. Brigid sent two of her nuns to ask for some of the wood. When Ailill refused, all the horses lay down and refused to rise even when the stakes and wattles were taken from their backs. It was only when Ailill offered all the loads to Brigid that the horses rose.

And so it was that Brigid built her church under an oak tree on a ridge above the Liffey plain. It was called *Cill Dara*, Irish for the "cell" or "church of the oak." Inside a circle of hedges beside the church, Brigid and her nuns kept a fire burning in honour of Christ, the light of the world. Surrounding the church were other buildings for cooking, sleeping, and the hosting of guests.

The poor came to be fed, the sick came to be healed, and, as always, if something was given to Brigid, she promptly gave it to someone who needed it more. Just as this charity had angered her father, her own nuns, who were often themselves in need of food and clothing, sometimes found it hard to bear.

Once a queen gave a beautiful silver chain to Brigid as an

offering. Now Brigid's nuns decided to hide it away until it could be of use to the community in a time of need. It wasn't long before Brigid came upon its hiding place, but she left it there as she had no use for it. The following day a leper came to beg alms of Brigid. Not having anything else, Brigid retrieved the chain and gave it to the man. When the nuns found out, they were bitterly angry, complaining that Brigid showed compassion to everyone but them. Brigid told them to go into the church to the place where she prayed. The nuns did so and found the chain there even though it had been given away. To trust as she did that God would provide must have been one of the great challenges of Brigid's community.

But Brigid cared deeply for the women who had dedicated themselves, as she had, to God. Knowing her own failings – a quick temper and lack of patience – she tried to be forgiving of the faults of those who lived with her. But there was one thing that Brigid would not tolerate – false piety. One time during Lent, Brigid's storehouse was almost empty. The last harvest of the year had not been good, and more and more people were coming to Brigid to be fed. Brigid had heard that a monastery some distance away had a supply of corn. Taking two of her nuns with her, Brigid set out. The entire countryside was suffering from near-famine and people, wretchedly thin, were digging roots for food. Tired and weak with hunger, Brigid and her companions finally reached their destination. The monastery had little food to offer them, but a kindly nun set a small amount of bread and bacon before them. Brigid asked the blessing and began to eat. Her companions ate the bread, but pushed the bacon aside.

"Is it not Lent?" one of them asked her.

Brigid stood up, knocking over the bench. "And what did our Lord say about the Pharisees and their show of holiness?" she asked.

People in the area surrounding Brigid's community became all too familiar with her request that all share what they had with those in need. Once Brigid came upon a neighbour carrying a sack. From the look of it, she guessed that it might hold salt, something her community was in need of to preserve meat for the coming winter.

"God be with you, good man," she said. "I'm wondering what it is you're carrying on this beautiful autumn day?"

"Stones," he said quickly, and hurried his pace.

"Stones it is," Brigid said.

The man's legs buckled under a sudden change in weight. He knew Brigid well, and, even though he had been hoping to avoid meeting her that day, his heart was in the right place. He couldn't help but laugh.

"What is that on your back?" Brigid asked again, unable to keep her own face serious.

"Salt," the man said. And so it was. Setting the bag on the ground, he dipped out a portion for Brigid.

On another lovely autumn day, a lady brought Brigid a present of her finest apples, carefully washed and beautifully arranged. Opening the basket, Brigid thanked the woman, commenting on the apples' sweet scent. Then she began to hand them out to a group of lepers who were standing nearby.

"I intended those as a present for you, not for the lepers," the lady said indignantly.

Brigid simply answered, "What is mine is theirs."

It was not just the poor and the sick who came to Brigid, the rich and powerful came as well. Once seven bishops came as a group to ask her advice. Her concern was that she had no food to give them, not even any milk as the cows had already been milked. Singing a prayer, Brigid herself, milked the cows for a third time. Her milking filled the tubs, and would have filled even all the vessels of Leinster, but, instead, the milk overflowed into a hollow that was called from that day on the 'Lake of Milk'.

Just as all her work was done in service to the Lord, who is God of all that is, the elements themselves responded to Brigid. One harvest time, when Brigid's granary was almost empty, rainstorms prevented the people from going out into the fields. Trusting, as always, that the Lord would hear her prayer, Brigid assembled a great band of reapers. On the appointed day, although rain poured down all over the Liffey plain, not a drop fell on her fields, and soon her granary was, again, full.

Like Saint Patrick, who helped with the ploughing and the other daily work of the people, Brigid took her turn tending the sheep. The silence of the broad pastureland was broken only by the sighing of the wind or the occasional bleating of a lamb for its mother. Undoubtedly its quiet was a welcome respite from the demands of her community. Perhaps it was there under the huge sky that she was best able to pray.

One day, as she was tending the sheep, a storm swept across the plain. By the time Brigid had hurried to a grove of trees, her cloak was dripping wet. Through the sheets of rain, a nun ran to her with the news that the great Brendan had come to visit and

Saint Brendan comes home

was waiting for her in the house. Brigid had heard stories of his adventures and she hurried to greet him.

Now Brendan had just spent seven years at sea. At one point on his journey, two frightening creatures had accompanied his boat, one mercilessly attacking the other. The victim called out to Saint Patrick and then to Brendan to save him, but it was not until the poor creature called upon the name of Brigid that the attacks ceased. Brendan resolved that when he returned home he would find out for himself how this Brigid could intercede so powerfully with God.

By the time Brigid arrived at the place where Brendan awaited her, the sun had come out again. In the darkness of the house, she mistook a shaft of sunlight for a roofbeam, and threw her wet cloak over it. Her dripping cloak hung there as neatly as if it were hung on the strongest rafter.

Brendan told his servant to put his cloak on the same ray, and the boy tried twice with no luck. Brendan angrily put it on a third time, and this time it stayed. Then Brendan asked Brigid to tell him how she went about serving God.

"You are my guest," she said. "I would like to hear your story first."

So Brendan said, "I hardly ever travel as far as seven ridges without thinking of God."

Then Brigid said, "Since I first gave myself to God, I have never taken my thoughts from Him."

And Brendan understood why all that she asked, and all that was asked in her name, was given.

The passing of years only made Brigid's desire to serve God stronger. And God was ever at hand – in the sky, the rivers, in all His creatures, be they birds or sheep, chieftains or lepers. She travelled the land, founding more churches, encouraging others, spreading the word of God. Always, she taught by example: that to serve Christ was to serve the poor, the sick, and the imprisoned. Always, she worked to make enemies friends, to bring peace to a warring land.

When age began to slow her steps, she still made the rounds of the area closest to Cill Dara. One afternoon, a messenger arrived to ask if she would visit the house of a local pagan chieftain who was surely near to breathing his last. Brigid, approaching the house, heard the man's fevered ravings. Although she was urged not to go in, she gently pushed aside the door covering and quietly seated herself on a stool by the man's bed. At once, he began to breathe more easily, and his eyes, at first so glassy and wild, began to calm. After Brigid gave him a sip of ale and wiped his brow, he sank back into his bed and closed his eyes.

Brigid picked up some rushes from those scattered on the floor. With hands, wrinkled with age, and worn and callused from work, she began to weave the rushes in and out, as she had done many times before. Looking up, she saw that the man was watching her.

"I am making a cross of rushes," she said, "in honour of Christ who died for us on a cross of wood."

As Brigid finished her weaving, she told the man the story of Jesus, how he had lived, suffered, and died so that everyone might have eternal life. Before the next dawn, when Brigid gently closed the man's eyes for the last time, he had been baptised.

At last, Brigid felt the ending of her days at hand. She asked to be carried to the highest place on the ridge. There, beside her beloved church, she looked out for the last time over the rolling land of her fields. The grass had just begun to green after the long winter, and she breathed deeply the rich earth smell of spring.

That night, the oldest of Brigid's nuns lit torches from the fire they had tended faithfully from the founding of *Cill Dara*. Reverently they followed her as she was carried into the church. With the glow of that fire illuminating her face, the time-carved lines melted away. Calling each by name, Brigid said farewell to those who had laboured with her to serve the Lord. Then she was anointed with the holy oil and received communion. A great peace, deep as the silence of her pastures, settled over all assembled. When the first red glow spread across the sky, she breathed her last.

As a shaft of sunlight lit up the grey stones of his room, a scribe wrote:

Always, this was her desire: to feed the poor, to repel every hardship, to be gentle to every misery… Towards God she was simple; towards the wretched she was compassionate; in miracles she was splendid… Therefore among created things she is like the Dove among birds, the Vine among trees, the Sun above stars… She is the Mary of the Gael.

And Brigid walks the land again whenever mercy is shown to those in need, whenever all are made welcome at the table, and when swords are exchanged for the food and drink of justice and peace.

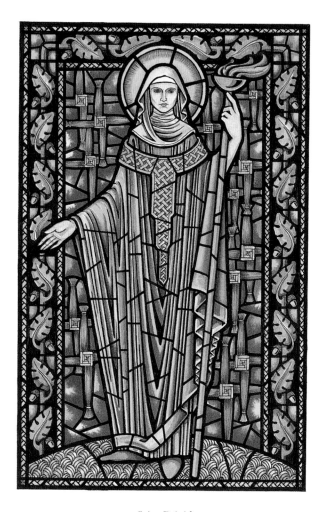

Saint Brigid

Chapter 2
Brigid – Goddess and Saint

As Christianity began to take root in Ireland, it assimilated many of the old pre-Christian Celtic beliefs and customs, in particular those dealing with the cycle of the seasons and rituals invoking protection and fertility. Living as she did during this time of transition, it is not surprising that the historical Brigid of Kildare was given attributes of her namesake Celtic goddess. This mixing of Celtic pre-Christian and Christian makes St Brigid a complex figure. There are some who would doubt her existence, saying she was the goddess Brigid made Christian. Others assert that she was an amalgam of many Brigids. But all would agree that St Brigid, second only to St Patrick, is a figure both revered and beloved. While her legends undeniably embody aspects of the goddess, they also tell of a woman who was a champion of the poor, a healer of the sick, and a peacemaker in a violent time. Lepers and beggars were as welcome at her table as the bishops and kings who sought her counsel. Her monastery at Kildare was, quite possibly, Ireland's first. It is seen by many as an historical testament to a woman of unique vision, personality, and spirit. Scholar Liam de Paor dates its founding at probably no later than 500 AD. As such, it is thought to predate monasteries founded by men.

Although we cannot be certain of the exact dates of Brigid's birth and death, the dates traditionally given – 453 to 524 AD – seem a good estimate given the monastery's founding date. Stories differ as to the place of her birth in Ireland. One story indicates that she was born in Faughart, two miles north of Dundalk, another that she was born not far from Kildare. Most stories tell that her father was a pagan chieftain named Dubhthach and her mother was Broicseach, his Christian slave.

The earliest written accounts of the saint, referred to as the Lives of Brigid, were composed in Latin in the seventh century. Cogitosus, who was probably a monk at the monastery of Kildare, wrote *Vita Brigitae* (Life of Brigid), which recounts multiple stories of the miraculous. Many, especially those involved with control of nature, are obvious adaptations of legends of the goddess, but he also includes stories of Brigid's generosity and compassion. He ends his account with a description of Brigid's church and the city that grew up around it. At a time when monasteries were vying with each other for power and prestige, his purpose in writing was probably to attract pilgrims to Kildare, one of the most important ecclesiastical centres in early Ireland.

The Old Irish *Life of St Brigid* tells us that she was accidentally consecrated a bishop. Her successor, the Abbess of Kildare did, indeed, seem to wield considerable authority, although a bishop acted as her coadjutor. When Brigid's monastery grew into a double monastery, where men and women lived in separate but adjacent buildings, the legends tell us that Brigid asked Conleth, a hermit and metal craftsman, to assist her.

Cogitosus's Latin account of the church at Kildare describes the body of Brigid laid to rest at the right of the high altar with Conleth's on the left. Both of their shrines were decorated with precious metals and jewels. A crown of gold hung above Brigid's shrine, a crown of silver above Conleth's. This ornate seventh-century church replaced earlier churches that were most probably constructed of timber, mud, and wattle.

Brigid's monastery at Kildare became renowned for its metalwork and illuminated manuscripts as well as for its hospitality and as a place of prayer. Devotion to the saint spread from Ireland to Scotland, Wales, Cornwall and the Isle of Man, as well as to Brittany and the wider Continent.

Brigid's Fire

Giraldus Cambrensis (Gerald of Wales) visited Kildare at the end of the 12th century. In his account of the visit, he described St Brigid's perpetual fire that had been kept burning throughout the centuries by her nuns. He told of how, in the time of Brigid, twenty nuns watched it in rotation, with Brigid herself watching it on the twentieth night. After her death, the number was not increased. Each nun kept the fire burning on her own night, and on the twentieth night the last nun put wood on the fire saying, "Brigid, keep your own fire, for the night has fallen to you." The fire was always still burning the following morning.

Research seems to indicate that, before the time of St Brigid, priestesses tended ritual fires on the 'Hill of Kildare' in honour of the goddess Brigid, asking her aid for good herds and crops. Archaeologists have dated a fire temple found near St Brigid's Cathedral in Kildare to pre-Christian times. On the north side of this 13th-century cathedral are the restored foundations of this temple. According to legend, St Brigid and her nuns re-consecrated this fire and kept it burning as a symbol of faith and a sign of their hospitality. Because of its pre-Christian associations, at least two bishops tried to do away with it, but it wasn't until the Reformation in the 16th century that the flame was finally extinguished. It was re-lit in 1993 by nuns of the Brigidine order and is kept burning as a perpetual flame.

The Goddess Brigid

The name Brigid is found in many forms – Brigit, Brighid, Brid; in Scotland as Bride, and in Wales as Ffraid. In Old Irish, it means "the exalted one" referring to the high place accorded Brigid among the Celtic goddesses. *Cormac's Glossary*, compiled in the ninth century by a monk of Cashel, Cormac MacCuilenan, identifies the pre-Christian Brigid as the principal goddess of Ireland. A daughter of the Dagda, she was a powerful protector-goddess worshipped by poets. Her sisters, also called Brigid, were goddesses of smith-work and healing. In this triad form, typical of Celtic gods, the goddess Brigid embodies characteristics of the ancient Mother Goddess in her aspects of wisdom, healing, nurturing, and protecting. In the various early writings describing Saint Brigid, these same qualities recur. The fire imagery associated with smith-work is also very evident in accounts of the saint.

The Celtic Goddess Brigid

Brigid's Feast Day and Imbolc

One of the most obvious links between the goddess and the saint is the date February 1st. That day, given in the Lives of Brigid as the day of St Brigid's death, is celebrated as St Brigid's Feast Day. It is also the date associated with the pre-Christian festival of Imbolc, a festival closely connected with the goddess Brigid.

In *Cormac's Glossary*, Imbolc is defined as 'the time the sheep's milk comes'. It was celebrated as the time of the earth's awakening after its long winter sleep. Rituals and talismans were used to encourage fertility and the abundant production of milk that people depended on for nourishment during this lean time of the year. Milk was associated with the nurturing aspect of the goddess and is frequently found in legends of the saint.

St Brigid's Day was traditionally the time to plant. Crops were sown in the warmer areas of the country. In northern places such as Donegal, the soil was prepared for planting. In all areas, people invoked Brigid's blessing, asking for good crops and an abundant harvest.

St Bride's Day in Scottish Folklore

Alexander Carmichael collected folklore in the Gaelic-speaking areas of the Scottish Highlands as well as the western islands of Scotland during the late 1800s. The *Carmina Gadelica* is the name of his collection of ancient prayers, blessings, invocations, charms, and songs, many of them associated with Brigid, known as St Bride in Scotland.

The following ancient hymn used to be sung to the serpent on St Bride's Day. The reference to the snake emerging from the ground after its winter hibernation probably symbolizes life emerging from the dead earth of winter:

> *On the day of Bride of the white hills,*
> *The noble queen will come from the knoll,*
> *I will not molest the noble queen,*
> *Nor will the noble queen molest me.*

In this excerpt, referring to the first of February, the saint embodies the goddess's power over nature:

> *Bride put her finger in the river*
> *On the feast day of Bride*
> *And away went the hatching mother of the cold...*

In another area of Scotland, Carmichael recorded the folk saying that Brigid "breathed life into the mouth of dead winter."

St Bride – Patroness of Knights

According to legend, St Bride was the patroness of the Knights of Chivalry who began calling the women they married their "brides." Possibly that is how the word found its way into the English language.

Chapter 3
St Brigid's Day Folk Customs

Folklorists have collected much of what we know about the rituals surrounding the celebration of St Brigid's Feast Day. Most of what has been collected in Ireland is housed in the archives of the National Folklore Collection at University College Dublin. *Festival of Brigid* is Séamus Ó Catháin's comprehensive study of this material.

Folklorist Padraigín Clancy identifies folk tradition as the place where the two Brigids – the goddess and the saint – meet. Milk and fire (symbols of the goddess), wells associated with her, and rituals performed during celebrations, in particular during Imbolc, gradually became interwoven with devotion to the saint. In traditional Irish culture, people trusted in Brigid's power to keep them safe. On St Brigid's Feast Day, and just as importantly on its eve, people performed many rituals through which they sought her protection for themselves, their families, their crops, and their livestock. Formerly widespread in Ireland and Scotland, Clancy notes a recent revitalisation of some customs, such as the making of the symbolic figure of Brigid that was carried from house to house (*brideog*), the Cloak or Mantle of Brigid (*Brat Bride*), and Brigid's Cross (*Cros Bride*).

St Brigid's Eve

Typically there were three parts to the St Brigid's Eve observance. First, Brigid was welcomed into the home. This was followed by a ceremonial meal in Brigid's honour, then the making of St Brigid's Cross/*Cros Bride*.

In many places, the father would go outside and knock at the door demanding entry in the name of Brigid. Often he would carry clothing wrapped around straw to represent the saint. The family, gathered inside, would joyously welcome the holy woman. This straw figure (*brideog*) would be put under the table during the meal, with the straw later used for crosses, ties, or, in some places, made into a bed for Brigid so she might spend the night. If any straw remained, it was spread in the stable to invoke fertility and protection.

In some villages, this welcoming of Brigid took the form of the *Brideog* procession where costumed boys and girls, Biddy Boys and Biddies, would go from house to house. In some places, only girls would take part. The leader of the group would carry a representation of Brigid. Often a peeled turnip, with eyes, nose, and mouth cut out and marked with soot, would serve as the head. The turnip would be put on a stick that would serve as the body and the whole would be wrapped in cloth. Sometimes the *brideog* was made of a churn dash dressed in clothes that were padded with stuffing. It was considered unlucky to turn away the young people carrying the *brideog*. In return for performing some type of entertainment, they would be given bread, cakes, eggs, or butter, which in some places would have been later used for a meal in one of the village's houses. In recent years, coins or sweets have been the gift for the costumed children. This custom is still observed in some places, especially in the west of Ireland.

Alexander Carmichael, the renowned Scottish folklorist, described this custom of the *brideog*, as it was traditionally carried out in the Gaelic speaking areas of Scotland, as primarily a female ritual. There, young girls made a figure of Bride out of a corn sheaf decorated with shells and early flowers with a bright stone placed on the breast. Then the girls, dressed in white with their hair down as a symbol of purity and youth, carried the figure from house to house, singing a song in honour of Bride. They were given the expected gifts to decorate the person of Bride by the people in the village. Mothers gave a Bride bannock (oatcake), a piece of cheese, or roll of butter. After receiving the gifts, the girls locked themselves in a house to which young men of the community came asking permission to enter so they might honour Bride. After much traditional parleying, they were finally admitted. The night passed in dancing and singing. In the morning, the remains of the feast were given to the poor.

In a striking illustration of Brigid's dual roles of both Virgin and Mother, the Gaelic mothers' ritual was significantly different than their daughters'. The mothers would make an oblong basket called the Bed of Bride. They, too, would make an image of Bride and decorate it. Then as recorded in Carmichael's *Carmina Gadelica*, '…one woman goes to the door of the house and, standing on the step with her hands on the jambs, calls softly into the darkness: "Bride's bed is ready." To this a ready woman behind replies: "Let Bride come in, Bride is welcome." The woman at the door again addresses Bride: "Bride, Bride, come thou in, thy bed is made. Preserve the house for the Trinity." The women then place the icon of Bride with great ceremony in the bed they have so carefully prepared for it.'

The ashes of the hearth were smoothed, hoping the saint would leave some telltale sign of her passing through the house during the night. In the early morning, the women anxiously scanned the ashes for Bride's footprint or the mark of her wand or finger. If a mark was found, the women rejoiced as it signified fertility in the family, the flocks, and the return of green life to the winter earth. If there was no trace, incense was burned and gifts offered. Traditionally, the gift was a cockerel buried alive near a place where three streams joined, and incense was burned on the hearth when the family went to bed.

These rituals, obviously ancient in origin, hearken back to times when they were regarded as necessary for fertility and protection, and perhaps, also, to aid the return of light and warmth, a rebirth of the earth itself.

St Brigid's Eve Meal

The second part of the St Brigid's Eve celebration was the meal held in the saint's honour. As she had been ceremoniously welcomed into the house, she was expected to be present at the table to share in the meal. The food itself was often just extra helpings of ordinary fare, but it was considered very important that butter be a part of the meal. As milk was scarce this time of the year, the woman of the house had to set a little aside every day in order to have enough to churn into butter. Remembering St Brigid's hospitality and concern for the poor, buttermilk with a lump of butter was traditionally given to the needy in order for them to properly celebrate the feast.

In some places *brúitín* or 'poundies' were the centrepiece of the meal. They were made of potatoes peeled, boiled, and mashed, mixed with onions and eaten with melted butter. In some areas, a sheaf of straw was placed on the floor under the pot of boiled and drained potatoes, and everyone in the house took a turn at pounding. This action, as well as the churning of butter, represented the fertility being evoked by many of the rituals associated with the feast.

A folkloric account from Donegal describes how the well-mashed poundies were placed in a large dish for the men of the house. A lump of butter, which quickly melted, was placed in a hole made in the centre. After a short prayer, the men made quick work of the meal scooping it out with their spoons, with often an extra spoon laid out for the saint. The women and the smaller children ate out of the pot, with butter added in the same way.

St Brigid's Cross / *Cros Bríde*

The third part of the St Brigid's Eve ritual was the making of St Brigid's crosses from the straw or rushes brought into the house earlier in the evening. Professor Ó Catháin notes that, in early times, women gave birth not in bed but on straw placed on the floor. This might help explain the connection of new life and fertility with straw.

Different types of crosses were made according to locality. The cross itself is an ancient symbol hearkening back to prehistoric times, possibly as a sun symbol. And, in one of its many aspects – as the tree of life, it represented fertility.

Legend tells us that while St Brigid visited the deathbed of a pagan chieftain, she wove a cross from the rushes that covered the floor. When he asked what she was doing, she told him the Gospel story and he asked to be baptised before he died.

Brigid's crosses are still made and placed inside homes above the door to ask the saint's protection from disease and fire. In older times, crosses would also be placed in the various outbuildings, to protect the animals and to promote the production of milk.

Brigidine sister Rita Minehan notes that, in some places, Brigid's cross was a symbol of goodwill, and was offered as an indication of a desire for peace after a local quarrel.

St Brigid's Girdle / *Crios Bride*

This representation of the saint's girdle was a circle made from a straw rope about twelve feet long. On the eve of the feast day, in what might be symbolic of birth, people would step through it. In some places, folk tradition tells of people passing through it three times, kissing it, and stepping out of it right foot first while reciting a prayer invoking Brigid's blessing. Unlike making the cross of St Brigid this ritual has all but disappeared.

St Brigid's Mantle or Cloak / *Brat Bride*

One of the most well known legends of St Brigid tells of how, when she needed land on which to build her monastery, she was told by the King that she could have what her cloak would cover. When she placed it on the ground, it miraculously expanded in all directions, and the King was forced to grant her the land she needed.

Traditionally, a piece of cloth, ribbon, or clothing was left outside on the eve of February 1st. It was thought that during the night St Brigid would touch this cloth as she passed by the house. This relic (*brat*) was later used for protection, healing, increasing fertility, and aiding both women and animals giving birth. Interestingly, it was also sometimes sewn into the clothing of young girls to protect their virginity.

Folk accounts are filled with stories of the *brat* being placed on the head of a woman experiencing a difficult labour, or being used to help cows calve. Sometimes the *brat* was placed over a cow to ensure a good supply of milk.

"The Mantle of Brigid upon you." (*Brat Bride Ort*), is a common Irish blessing that invokes the protection of the saint. Ireland, itself, is sometimes referred to as "Brigid's Green Mantle."

Live Shellfish / *Iasc Beo*

Folklorist Clancy describes this custom of placing live shellfish in the four corners of the home on St Brigid's Day as a ritual still found in parts of the Aran Islands. This was done to ensure good fishing, which would bring the family prosperity during the coming year. Some of the shellfish used in this ritual, such as barnacles and limpets, reproduce from eggs without benefit of fertilisation. This is, again, a link to the fertility symbolism of the goddess Brigid.

Food Offerings

Sometimes a saucer of milk or a small portion of butter, cake, or bread might be put outside on the windowsill as an offering to the saint as she passed by on the eve of her feast day.

Chapter 4
St Brigid the Aid-Woman

St Brigid's Wells

Wells dedicated to St Brigid are found all over Ireland. Legends associated with some of them tell of the saint stopping by the well on one of her many journeys throughout the land, blessing the water, and, in some places, using it to heal. On the outskirts of Kildare there are two holy wells. The "wayside well" near the Japanese Gardens is thought to be pre-Christian. At nearby Tully, water from a spring runs through a channel with two holed stones, possibly representing the breasts of the saint, and thus symbolic of milk and fertility. Another St Brigid's well is at Faughart, north of Dundalk, in Co. Louth, according to many of the legends, the birthplace of the saint. The most visited of all the St Brigid wells is probably the one at Liscannor, Co. Clare, where pilgrim offerings ranging from statues to crutches, hand-written notes to ribbons and coins line the walls of the passage that leads down to the well. Everything the visitors leave behind represents something, possibly a favour asked or perhaps as a token of thanksgiving.

In pre-Christian times, wells were seen as sacred places, as entrances to mother earth. Exiting wells such as the one at Liscannor, coming from the darkness into the light, quite possibly signified birth. The waters of the holy wells were said to have healing properties. Some wells such as the one at Kilbride (*Cill Bhríde*) near Ballycastle, Co. Mayo and Brideswell (*Tobar Bhríde*) in Co. Roscommon were said to cure sterility.

Rag or clootie trees are found near many holy wells. A clootie is a symbol of the request someone has made. It is usually a piece of cloth, although it might also be a ribbon, shoe lace, piece of paper, or other item. It is tied to a tree, often a hazel, whitethorn, or ash, near the well.

St Brigid as the Virgin Mary's Helper and Patroness of Midwives

Reflecting the Celtic belief in 'thin places' where the boundaries between the world of time and the world of eternity were permeable, there is a tradition that identifies St Brigid as the mid-wife who helped Mary give birth to Christ. An account in the *Carmina Gadelica* describes how Brigid was a serving maid at the inn in Bethlehem when Mary and Joseph came looking for a place to stay. Sad that she could not give them shelter, she did give them water and some of her own bannock. Later that night, when she saw a brilliant light over the door of the stable, she went and assisted Mary, receiving the baby in her arms. This is why in the Scottish Highlands when a woman was in labour the midwife would go to the door and standing on the doorstep with her hands on the jamb would beseech Brigid to come saying, "Bride! Bride! Come in, Thy welcome is truly made."

In this prayer from the *Carmina Gadelica*, the woman in labour asked for Brigid's aid:

Bride – the Aid-Woman

There came to me assistance
Mary fair and Bride;
As Anna bore Mary,
As Mary bore Christ,
As Eile bore John the Baptist
Without flaw in him,
Aid thou me in mine unbearing,
Aid me, O Bride!

As Christ was conceived of Mary
Full perfect on every hand,
Assist thou me, foster-mother,
The conception to bring from the bone;
And as thou didst aid the Virgin of joy,
Without gold, without corn, without kine,
Aid thou me, great is my sickness,
Aid me, O Bride!

Candlemas / Feast of Purification

Irish legends tell how Brigid walked before Mary with a lighted candle in each hand as Mary went up to the temple to be purified after Christ's birth. Although a strong wind blew, the flames of Brigid's candles never wavered.

Wonderful in its mix of conversational tone and vivid pre-Christian imagery, Séamas Ó Catháin cites the following account from the folklore of Co. Galway as representative of a traditional Irish legend of Brigid aiding Mary:

'The Blessed Virgin was about to be 'churched' and as she was going to the church, she met St Brigid. Our Blessed Lady was very shy in going to the altar rails before the whole congregation and she told Brigid how she felt. "Never mind," says Brigid, "I'll manage that part all right." She got a harrow and put it on her head turning the points upwards. They went into the church and no sooner had St Brigid entered than every point of the harrow turned into a lighted candle. The whole congregation turned their eyes on St Brigid and her crown of lighted candles and the Blessed Virgin proceeded to the altar rails and not an eye was turned on her until the ceremony was over. The Blessed Virgin was so delighted with St Brigid that she gave her her day before her own and that is the reason that St Brigid's Day is before the feast of the Purification.'

This extract is taken from the National Folklore Collection held at University College Dublin (NFC902:187-188)

It is interesting to note that Brigid, linked with the Virgin in such intimate ways in folk tradition, is known to this day as Mary of the Gael (*Muire na nGael*), and that a customary greeting is:

> "Brigid and Mary be with you"
> (*Brid is Muire dhuit*).

In addition to aiding midwives, Brigid was said to help cure ailments as the following incantation found in the *Carmina Gadelica* records:

Charm of the Sprain

*Bride went out
In the morning early,*

With a pair of horses;
One broke his leg,
With much ado,
That was apart,
She put bone to bone,
She put flesh to flesh,
She put sinew to sinew,
She put vein to vein;
As she healed that
May I heal this.

Chapter 5
Traditional Prayers to St Brigid

The following five prayers are from the *Carmina Gadelica*, Alexander Carmichael's collection of folklore from the Gaelic-speaking areas of the Scottish Highlands and the western islands of Scotland. Carmichael worked in that area as an employee of the United Kingdom's Civil Service, but his passion was collecting and preserving the rich folk tradition that he found there. As he went out among the people he won their trust and friendship. Thus he was able to collect, and subsequently translate, the Gaelic hymns, charms, and prayers that were on the verge of extinction.

This great invocation of Brigid, the *Genealogy of Bride*, is a prayer for protection that begins with a recitation of Brigid's ancestors.

Genealogy of Bride

The genealogy of the holy maiden Bride,
Radiant flame of gold, noble foster-mother of Christ.
Bride the daughter of Dugall the brown,
Son of Aodh, son of Art, son of Conn,
Son of Crearar, son of Cis, son of Carmac, son of Carruin.

Every day and every night
That I say the genealogy of Bride,
I shall not be killed, I shall not be harried,
I shall not be put in cell, I shall not be wounded,

Recording Saint Brigid's Life

Neither shall Christ leave me in forgetfulness.
No fire, no sun, no moon shall burn me,
No lake, no water, nor sea shall drown me,
No arrow of fairy nor dart of fay shall wound me,
And I under the protection of my Holy Mary,
And my gentle foster-mother is my beloved Bride.

The following invocation asked the saints and angels for protection:

The Cross of the Saints and the Angels

The cross of the saints and of the angels with me
From the top of my face to the edge of my soles.

O Michael mild, O Mary of glory,
O gentle Bride of the locks of gold,
Preserve ye me in the weakly body,
The three preserve me on the just path.
Oh! three preserve me on the just path.

Preserve ye me in the soul-shrine poor,
Preserve ye me, and I so weak and naked,
Preserve ye me without offence on the way,
The preservation of the three upon me tonight.
Oh! the three to shield me tonight.

Many prayers asked for blessings on work – kindling the fire in the morning as well as banking, or smooring, the fire at night, milking, herding, sowing, reaping, weaving, hunting and fishing. In the following prayer, Brigid's protection was invoked by the woman of the house as she smoored the fire before going to bed. In this necessary nightly ritual, the coals were covered with ash to keep them burning during the night so that a new fire would not have to be lit in the morning.

Smooring the Fire

I will build the hearth,
As Mary would build it.
The encompassment of Bride and of Mary,
Guarding the hearth, guarding the floor,
Guarding the household all.

Who are they on the lawn without?
Michael the sun-radiant of my trust.
Who are they on the middle of the floor?
John and Peter and Paul.
Who are they by the front of my bed?
Sun-bright Mary and her Son.

The mouth of God ordained,
The angel of God proclaimed,
An angel white in charge of the hearth
'Til white day shall come to the embers.
An angel white in charge of the hearth
'Til white day shall come to the embers.

Herding Blessing

I will place this flock before me,
As was ordained of the King of the world,
Bride to keep them, to watch them, to tend them,
On ben, on glen, on plain,
Bride to keep them, to watch them, to tend them,
On ben, on glen, on plain.

Arise, thou Bride the gentle, the fair,
Take thou thy lint, thy comb, and thy hair,
Since thou to them madest the noble charm,
To keep them from straying, to save them from harm,
Since thou to them madest the noble charm,
To keep them from straying, to save them from harm.

From rocks, from drifts, from streams,
From crooked passes, from destructive pits,
From the straight arrows of the slender banshee,
From the heart of envy, from the eye of evil,
From the straight arrows of the slender banshee,
From the heart of envy, from the eye of evil.

Mary Mother, tend thou the offspring all,
Bride of the fair palms, guard thou my flocks,
Kindly Columba, thou saint of many powers,
Encompass thou the breeding cows, bestow on me herds,
Kindly Columba, thou saint of many powers,
Encompass thou the breeding cows, bestow on me herds.

St Bride's Charm

The charm put by Bride the beneficent,
On her goats, on her sheep, on her kine,
On her horses, on her chargers, on her herds,
Early and late going home, and from home.

To keep them from rocks and ridges,
From the heels and the horns of one another,
From the birds of the Red Rock,
And from Luath of the Feinne.

From the blue peregrine hawk of Creag Duilion,
From the brindled eagle of Ben-Ard,
From the swift hawk of Tordun,
From the surly raven of Bard's Creag.

From the fox of the wiles,
From the wolf of the Mam,
From the foul-smelling fumart,
And from the restless great-hipped bear.

From…
From…
From every hoofed of four feet,
And from every hatched of two wings.

The final verse allowed the reciters to personalise the words to their own circumstances.

Other Traditional Prayers

Brigid was said to have aided the Virgin Mary with her child, so it is not surprising that Irish mothers asked for her help and protection, as in this traditional prayer, as they put their own children to bed at night.

> *May God bless you, child.*
> *I put you under the protections of Mary and her Son,*
> *Under the care of Brigid and her cloak,*
> *And under the shelter of God tonight.*

The following is a traditional Irish table grace often referred to as *St Brigid's Ale Soliloquy.* Legends of the saint are filled with tales of her hospitality and her concern that all be well fed.

Brigid's Feast

> *I should like a great lake of finest ale*
> *For the King of Kings.*
> *I should like a table of the choicest food*
> *For the family of heaven.*
> *Let the ale be made of the fruits of faith,*
> *And the food be forgiving love.*
>
> *I should welcome the poor to my feast,*
> *For they are God's children.*
> *I should welcome the sick to my feast,*
> *For they are God's joy.*
> *Let the poor sit with Jesus at the highest place,*
> *And the sick dance with the angels.*

God bless the poor,
God bless the sick,
And bless our human race.
God bless our food,
God bless our drink,
All homes, O God, embrace.

And finally, a traditional prayer said by Irish emigrants bidding farewell to their native land:

The Emigrant's Prayer

Brigid that is in Faughart
Blinne that is in Killeavey
Bronagh that is in Ballinakill
May you bring me back to Ireland.

Chapter 6
St Brigid Today

With the burgeoning interest in Celtic spirituality, one might say that St Brigid has been rediscovered. People searching for ways to experience and celebrate their connection to a reality where everything is sacred are drawn to the figure of Brigid, who saw all life as holy, who prayed always in all ways. In her connection to the ancient Celtic goddess, she embodied so much that was elemental, intimately connected to the natural world. At the same time, legends of the saint show her as a courageous woman confronting issues of her day – poverty, inequality, injustice, and war, in parables applicable to our own times. It is no wonder that Brigid, a figure who bridged very different worlds, resonates with people of today.

In 1993 Brigid's fire was rekindled in Kildare's Market Square. Reflecting the concerns of the saint, it was appropriately lit by the leader of the Brigidine Sisters at the opening of a peace and justice conference. *Solas Bhríde* (Brigid's Light) is the sisters' Christian centre for Celtic Spirituality in Kildare. Brigid's fire is kept burning there as well as in the Market Square at Kildare. The city's *Féile Bríde* (Festival of Brigid) is a multi-faceted event that lasts for several days and is a combination of pilgrimage, peace and justice conference, lectures, and music. Open to all, it is organised by the Brigidine Sisters, *Cáirde Bhríde* (Friends of Brigid), and AFRI (Action from Ireland).

Saint Brigid's legacy continues

Just as the hospitality of the saint's monastery drew people from all over Ireland, so the spirit of Brigid continues to attract people to Kildare. Pilgrims come to walk in her footsteps and to dip hands into the cool waters of her holy wells. When they return home, some symbolically and others literally, carry the flame of Brigid with them.

Chapter 7
Making a St Brigid's Cross

Just as the shamrock is associated with St Patrick, a cross made from rushes is the symbol of St Brigid. This is one of the most widespread Irish customs associated with her. Legend tells how she picked up rushes from the floor and began to weave them into a cross while she sat at the deathbed of a pagan chieftain. When he asked what she was doing, she told him about Jesus and his death on the cross. Before he died, the chieftain asked to be baptised.

Crosses are traditionally made from rushes, but they can also be made from wheat stalks, grasses, or reeds. If the reeds or rushes are dry and brittle, soak them to soften them.

The crosses are typically made on the eve of St Brigid's Day and placed above the door of the house for blessing and protection.

Directions:

1.   Hold one reed vertically, and fold another in half around the mid-point of the first.

2.   Take a third reed and fold it around the second one, parallel to the first. You should now have a T-shaped piece, with one arm having one strand, another having two and the third having three.

3. Fold a fourth reed around the third one to form a cross.

4. Fold a fifth one around the fourth, parallel to the single strand. As you work, snug the reeds against the centre and hold it tight.

5. Continue folding reeds around the previous one (and the ones beside it) working in a circular fashion until you have created enough of a woven centre.

6. When the centre is as big as you like, hold the reeds together carefully and tie the ends of each arm tightly with reeds, string or some type of natural fibre. Trim the ends with scissors.

A traditional blessing said in some parts of Ireland for the hanging of St Brigid's cross:

"May the blessing of God and the Trinity be on this cross, and on the home where it hangs and on everyone who looks at it."

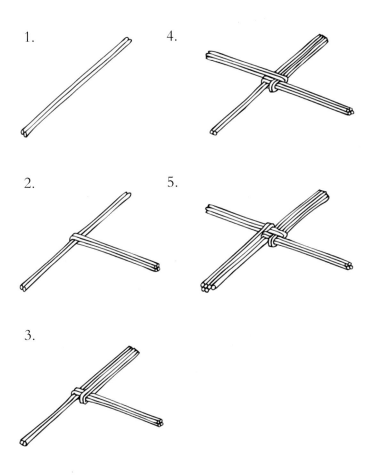

1.

2.

3.

4.

5.

Repeat steps 2–5 twice and tie up ends with reeds or string.
Finally trim the ends

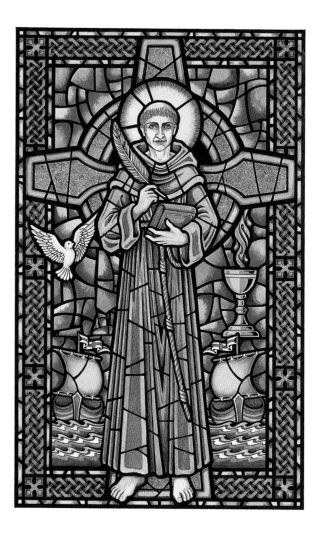

Sources

For my telling of St Brigid's story, I have used the *Leabhar Breac*, otherwise known as the *Speckled Book of the MacEgans* as my primary source. A scribe copying manuscripts dating back to the tenth century or earlier wrote it in Middle Irish in the early 15th century. Vivid in its descriptions, it was written to preserve material of religious concerns. I used the translation of the *Leabhar Breac* by Whitley Stokes, printed in 1877 as "Three Middle-Irish Homilies on the Lives of Saints Patrick, Brigit and Columba." In the tradition of the manuscripts themselves, where longer narratives often replaced mere listings, I have taken the liberty to imaginatively reconstruct the incidents described in the *Leabhar Breac*.

The incidents and legends listed below from other accounts were too wonderful to leave out of St Brigid's story:

The greening of the altar post in the consecration of Brigid p. 64; the playing of the harps pp. 94-95; the gift of apples pp. 105-106; and the nuns' false piety during Lent pp. 138-139 – *St Brigid of Ireland* by Alice Curtayne, Dublin: Brown and Nolan, Ltd., 1933.

Brigid's cloak pulled by four of her nuns expands to cover the Curragh p. 334 – *Legendary Fictions of the Irish Celts* by Patrick Kennedy, London: Macmillan, 1866; reissued by New York/London: Benjamin Bloom, 1969.

The folklore account from County Galway of how St Brigid aided the Virgin Mary is taken from the National Folklore Collection held at University College Dublin. The extract (NFC902 187-188) is reproduced with kind permission of the Head of UCD school for Irish, Celtic Studies, Irish folklore and Lingistics.

The Traditional Prayers to St Brigid (as acknowledged) are from the *Carmina Gadelica*, Alexander Carmichael's great collection of folklore, prayers, blessings, invocations, charms, and songs, from the oral tradition of Gaelic-speakers in the Scottish Highlands and the western islands of Scotland during the late 1800s. Published by the Scottish Academic Press under the title *Carmina Gadelica, Hymns and Incantations Orally Collected in the Highlands and Islands of Scotland and Translated into English*, the entire work is comprised of six volumes published under different editors. Volumes I and II were edited by Alexander Carmichael and published in 1900. The items from the *Carmina Gadelica* used in this book are from those first two volumes. All six volumes are now available in a single book published for non-Gaelic speakers in 1992 by Floris Books.

The following books have been used as sources of additional prayers:

A Little Book of Irish Blessings written by Pat Fairon and published by Appletree Press, Belfast, in 1992 (pp. 44 and 60).

A Little Book of Irish Toasts published by Appletree Press, Belfast, in 1987 (p. 57).

Acknowledgements

For help in understanding the Folk Customs of Brigid's Eve and Day, I wish to acknowledge the following sources:

Two essays in *Celtic Threads*, Padraigín Clancy, ed. Dublin: Veritas Publications, 1999: "Brigid: Muire Na nGael (Mary of the Gael)" by Padraigín Clancy, pp. 33-49 and "Kildare Today: Continuing the Brigidine Tradition" by Mary Minehan, pp. 161-170.

Séamas Ó Catháin's article "The Festival of Brigit the Holy Woman" in *Celtica* 23, pp. 231-260, School of Celtic Studies DIAS 1999.

Rekindling the Flame – A Pilgrimage in the Footsteps of Brigid of Kildare by Rita Minehan, CSB, published by Solas Bhríde Community, 14 Dara Park, Kildare, Ireland, 1999.